Connecticut

Jim Ollhoff

Visit us at
www.abdopublishing.com

Published by ABDO Publishing Company, 8000 West 78th Street, Suite 310, Edina, Minnesota 55439 USA. Copyright ©2010 by Abdo Consulting Group, Inc. International copyrights reserved in all countries. No part of this book may be reproduced in any form without written permission from the publisher. The Checkerboard Library™ is a trademark and logo of ABDO Publishing Company.

Printed in the United States.

Editor: John Hamilton
Graphic Design: Sue Hamilton
Cover Illustration: Neil Klinepier
Cover Photo: iStock Photo
Interior Photo Credits: Alamy, AP Images, Comstock, Connecticut Sun, Corbis, David Olson, Getty, Granger Collection, Gunter Küchler, iStock Photo, Library of Congress, Matt Mioduszewski, Mile High Maps, Moby, Mountain High Maps, NASA, North Wind Picture Archives, One Mile Up, University of Connecticut Huskies, and the University of Wisconsin Milwaukee.
Statistics: State population statistics taken from 2008 U.S. Census Bureau estimates. City and town population statistics taken from July 1, 2007, U.S. Census Bureau estimates. Land and water area statistics taken from 2000 Census, U.S. Census Bureau.

Manufactured with paper containing at least 10% post-consumer waste

Library of Congress Cataloging-in-Publication Data

Ollhoff, Jim, 1959-
  Connecticut / Jim Ollhoff.
       p. cm. -- (The United States)
  Includes index.
  ISBN 978-1-60453-642-3
  1. Connecticut--Juvenile literature. I. Title.

  F94.3.O44 2010
  974.6--dc22

                              2008051027

Table of Contents

Constitution State...4

Quick Facts 6

Geography 8

Climate and Weather 12

Plants and Animals...14

History...18

Did You Know?...24

People 26

Cities 30

Transportation...34

Natural Resources 36

Industry...38

Sports 40

Entertainment...42

Timeline...44

Glossary...46

Index...48

Constitution State

Connecticut is a land of small towns. The towns are built around village greens and churches with high steeples. Rolling hills and forests extend as far as the eye can see.

The state has many factories. Because of this, there used to be a lot of pollution. In the 1980s and 1990s, laws were passed to keep the state clean. Efforts to clean up the land and water have been very successful.

Connecticut's nickname is the "Constitution State." In 1638, the Connecticut colony created the Fundamental Orders. This united the cities and villages. Connecticut was the first American colony to use this type of written constitution. Nearly 150 years later, historians believe this document may have been used by America's Founding Fathers to help them write the United States Constitution.

Connecticut is known for its beautiful
fall colors and steepled churches.

Name: May be from a Mohegan Indian word, *quinnehtukqut*, meaning "place of the long river," which refers to the Connecticut River.

State Capital: Hartford, population 124,563

Date of Statehood: January 9, 1788 (5th state)

Population: 3,501,252 (29th-most populous state)

Area (Total Land and Water): 5,543 square miles (14,356 sq km), 48th-largest state

Largest City: Bridgeport, population 136,695

Nickname: The Constitution State

Motto: *Qui Transtulit Sustinet* (He Who Transplanted Still Sustains)

State Bird: American Robin

State Flower: Mountain Laurel

State Mineral: Garnet

State Tree: White or Charter Oak

State Song: "Yankee Doodle"

Highest Point: Mount Frissell, 2,380 feet (725 m)

Lowest Point: The shore of Long Island Sound, 0 feet (0 m)

Average July Temperature: 72°F (22°C)

Mount Frissell

Record High Temperature: 106°F (41°C), on July 15, 1995, at Danbury

Average January Temperature: 26°F (-3°C)

Record Low Temperature: -32°F (-36°C), on February 16, 1943, at Falls Village

Long Island Sound

Average Annual Precipitation: 45 inches (114 cm)

Number of U.S. Senators: 2

Number of U.S. Representatives: 5

U.S. Presidents Born in Connecticut: George W. Bush (43rd president)

George W. Bush

U.S. Postal Service Abbreviation: CT

Geography

Connecticut is the third-smallest state. It is located in the northeast corner of the United States, in a region called New England. The region of New England consists of the states of Maine, Vermont, New Hampshire, Massachusetts, Rhode Island, and Connecticut.

Long Island Sound.

The state is almost the shape of a rectangle. In the southwest corner, there is a panhandle extending toward New York City. Connecticut has Massachusetts to the north, Rhode Island to the east, and New York to the west. On the south side of the state is a bay of water called Long Island Sound.

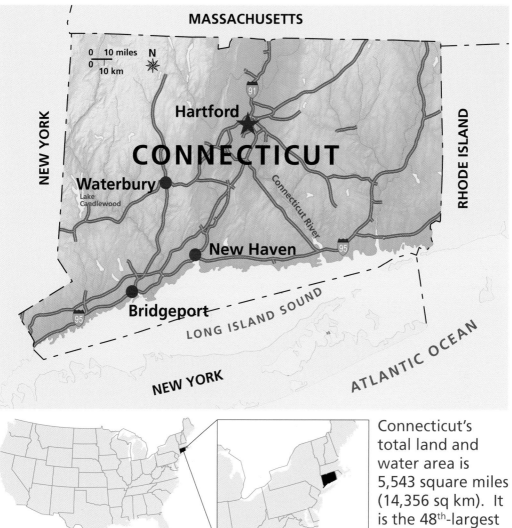

MASSACHUSETTS

0   10 miles
0   10 km

N

NEW YORK

RHODE ISLAND

Hartford

CONNECTICUT

Waterbury

Lake Candlewood

Connecticut River

New Haven

Bridgeport

LONG ISLAND SOUND

NEW YORK

ATLANTIC OCEAN

Connecticut's total land and water area is 5,543 square miles (14,356 sq km). It is the 48th-largest state. The state capital is Hartford.

Although the state is small, it has many people. It was settled early in the history of the United States because of its good soil. It is located along the Atlantic Coast, which is a good location for fishing and trading.

At 407 miles (655 km), the Connecticut River is the longest river in New England. Dutch explorers traveled up the river in the early 1600s. Europeans first settled land along the Connecticut River. The largest lake in the state is Lake Candlewood.

The Connecticut River is used by large and small watercraft.

A hiker on Bear Mountain.

Residents argue about the highest place in Connecticut. Bear Mountain rises to 2,354 feet (717 m) above sea level. Mount Frissell is higher, but the actual top of Mount Frissell is in Massachusetts. The southern slope of Mount Frissell is 2,380 feet (725 m), and the southern slope is in Connecticut. So, the highest mountain in Connecticut is Bear Mountain. The highest point in Connecticut is the southern slope of Mount Frissell.

Climate and Weather

Connecticut has warm summers and cool winters. The Atlantic Ocean keeps the climate mild. Spring and autumn are very pleasant. The beautifully colored fall trees bring many visitors to the state in October and November.

A blast of beautiful fall color in Connecticut.

Snowfall ranges from 25–100 inches (64–254 cm) in winter. Most of the snow falls in the northwest part of the state. For most of the winter, temperatures are above freezing.

Summer temperatures average 80 to 88 degrees Fahrenheit (27–31°C). The temperature goes over 90 degrees Fahrenheit (32°C) only about 12 days a year.

While most hurricanes occur in warmer southern areas, sometimes hurricanes can go north toward Connecticut. Tornadoes can occasionally be threatening, especially in the Connecticut River Valley. Thunderstorms are more common. About 30 storms strike each summer.

Lightning strikes open water during a summer storm on Long Island Sound.

Plants and Animals

Before Connecticut was settled by Europeans, it was completely forested. Today, about 60 percent of the state is forest. The common trees are beech, maple, oak, and birch. Hemlock and white pine are found throughout the state. The white or charter oak is the state tree.

The most common animals in the state are rabbit, chipmunk, squirrel, muskrat, otter, fox, skunk, and woodchuck. Deer were once almost gone from the state, but have made a comeback. Coyotes still prowl the state. Bear and wolves, once common, no longer live in Connecticut.

Two young skunks.

Red Fox

Whitetail Buck

Woodchucks

A red-bellied woodpecker.

A North American blue jay.

There are almost 300 species of birds in the state. Blue jay, woodpecker, sparrow, goldfinch, chickadee, hawk, and crow are common. The robin is Connecticut's state bird. Game birds include grouse, duck, and pheasant.

Many kinds of fish live in Long Island Sound, directly south of the state. Clams and oysters are numerous. Striped bass, flounder, butterfish, blackfish, and bluefish are common ocean fish. In the freshwater rivers and lakes, perch, bass, bluegill, bullhead, and trout are found.

A clam.

Common bushes and shrubs include wild cherry, sweet fern, huckleberry, and blueberry. Wildflowers include violet, bloodroot, jack-in-the-pulpit, and cowslip. The mountain laurel is the state flower.

Blueberry Bush   Bloodroot Flowers   Jack-in-the-Pulpit   Mountain Laurel

History

Before the arrival of Europeans in the early 1600s, many Native American tribes lived in the area. About 16 different tribes lived in Connecticut, including the Mohegan, Nipmuc, Hammonasset, Quinnipiac, and others. The Pequot tribe was probably the most powerful. They hunted and fished. They grew pumpkins, corn, beans, squash, and other crops. "Connecticut" is from the Mohegan word *quinnehtukqut.* It means "place of the long river," referring to the Connecticut River.

A Dutch explorer named Adriaen Block sailed up the Connecticut River in 1614. The Dutch established a trading post near present-day Hartford.

The first permanent settlers were the English. They came from Massachusetts in 1635. Led by John Winthrop, they settled south of Hartford. Other groups of English colonists later settled around the state. The Connecticut colony had begun.

John Winthrop meets with a Native American.

For most of Connecticut's early history, relationships between the colonists and the Native Americans were good. One big battle was the Pequot War in 1637–1638. The Pequot people defended their land, but were nearly wiped out by the colonists.

In 1637, Captain John Mason led English colonists against the Pequot tribe near Stonington, Connecticut.

In the 1700s, tension between England and the American colonies grew. Finally, the American colonies declared their independence from England. Connecticut was of great importance during the Revolutionary War. Factories in Connecticut furnished the American military with guns and other supplies. Connecticut soldiers fought in most of the important battles of the war.

Connecticut representatives helped to write the Declaration of Independence and the Constitution of the United States. Connecticut became the fifth state in the United States on January 9, 1788.

Benjamin Franklin, John Adams, and Thomas Jefferson read a draft of the Declaration of Independence.

Agriculture and manufacturing continued to power the state through the 1800s. In 1848, Connecticut abolished

Cannons are manned by soldiers of the 1st Connecticut Heavy Artillery during the Civil War.

slavery. During the Civil War, the state supported the Union North. Connecticut sent more than 50,000 troops to fight in the Civil War.

By the early 1900s, Connecticut was expanding its industry. It continued to manufacture and sell metal products, brassware, clocks, and other items. During World War I, the state's factories provided many of the weapons that soldiers used.

The Great Depression began in 1929. It was a difficult time when people all over the United States were jobless. Money was scarce and many Americans could barely keep food on the table.

World War II helped the Connecticut economy. There were orders for weapons and other products from Connecticut factories. Submarines were built in Connecticut, as well as aircraft parts, parachutes, and machine parts.

In 1943, two workers paint a sub's hatch at the Electric Boat Company in Groton, Connecticut.

After World War II, Connecticut went through many changes. The state became home to several insurance companies. Some large businesses moved out of the state. African American and Hispanic populations increased. A few Native American tribes settled land disputes. Throughout its history, Connecticut has changed and grown. It continues to do so today.

Did You Know?

Roger Sherman

A Connecticut statesman came up with an idea that helped create the United States government. It was known as the Connecticut Compromise.

Early in the history of the United States, state representatives gathered for a Constitutional Convention. The year was 1787, and the representatives had to decide how the federal government should be run. Everyone wanted legislators to represent their state. However, the larger states wanted congressional representation by size of population. The smaller states wanted equal representation for each state, no matter what its population. The convention was deadlocked.

Then, a Connecticut statesman named Roger Sherman, and a few others, came up with a plan called the Connecticut Compromise. The plan called for a Congress made up of two sections. One part would be the House of Representatives. It would have a number of representatives based on the population of each state. The other part would be the Senate. Each state would have two senators, no matter what the state's population. To pass a law, both parts of Congress would have to agree on it.

The Connecticut Compromise saved the Constitutional Convention. Roger Sherman's plan is still used in the United States Congress.

Roger Sherman led the work on the Connecticut Compromise.

People

Prudence Crandall (1803–1890) was a schoolteacher who fought hard for African Americans. In the early 1800s, in many places it was against the law to educate people of color. In 1833, she opened a school for African American women in Canterbury, Connecticut. The school faced threats and violence. She was arrested. Although charges were dropped, attacks on her school caused her to close it in 1834. However, four years later, her work changed Connecticut laws. In 1838, African Americans were allowed an education. In 1995, Prudence Crandall was named Connecticut's official state heroine.

Roger Sherman (1721–1793) was a judge and statesman. He helped write the Articles of Confederation, and he signed the Declaration of Independence. When the Constitutional Convention was held, Sherman helped to create a compromise that made the convention a success.

Benedict Arnold (1741–1801) was born in Norwich, Connecticut. He led several successful battles against the British during the Revolutionary War. He even defended Danbury, Connecticut, from a British attack. However, he was not good at dealing with people. The military promoted others. Arnold began telling American military secrets. He led British troops against his old friends. Down through history, the name of "Benedict Arnold" has been another word for "traitor."

Nathan Hale (1755–1776) was born in Coventry, Connecticut. He was a graduate of Yale College, and a schoolteacher. He joined the American forces in 1775 as they fought to gain independence from Great Britain. In 1776, he snuck behind enemy lines to gather information on the British, but he was caught and hanged. He is remembered for the speech he gave before he was executed. He reportedly said, "I only regret that I have but one life to lose for my country." In 1985, Connecticut made Nathan Hale the official hero of the state.

Nathan Hale fought for America's independence.

Musician and record producer **Moby** (1965–) was born in New York, but grew up in Darien, Connecticut. He began making music when he was nine, first learning classical guitar. Moby went on to play in a punk band, and in the 1990s became famous for his style of techno dance music. His real name is Richard Melville Hall. Moby became his nickname because he is related to author Herman Melville, who wrote the classic story *Moby-Dick*.

Author **Stephenie Meyer** (1973-) was born in Hartford, Connecticut. Her family moved to Arizona when she was young. Meyer majored in English in college. Her first books, the *Twilight* vampire-based fantasy series, have made her one of today's most popular authors.

Cities

Bridgeport sits along the coast in the southwest corner of the state. Before the Europeans came in 1639, the area was a Pequannock Indian village. Europeans established the town in 1821. With a deep harbor, it became a place for fishing and shipbuilding. Today, with 136,695 people, it is the largest city in Connecticut. The city is known for manufacturing and banking. The University of Bridgeport has its home in this city.

The city of **Hartford** sits in the center of the state, along the Connecticut River. It is the capital of Connecticut. Its population is 124,563.

The Sicaog, a Native American tribe, lived in the area before the Europeans came. The Dutch established a trading post in the early 1620s. English settlers arrived soon afterward. Today, the city is known as the "insurance capital of the world." Many major insurance companies have their headquarters in Hartford. The city is also home to several colleges, including the University of Hartford and the Hartford Conservatory.

New Haven is a port city on Long Island Sound. The Puritans from England settled the area in 1638. It began as a collection of several cities, with its own governor. In 1664, it became part of the Connecticut colony. New Haven grew in importance because of its many manufacturing companies. The famous Yale University is located in this city. New Haven's population is 123,932.

Downtown
New Haven has many old buildings.

Yale University was founded in 1701. So far, five United States presidents have graduated from Yale.

The fifth-largest town in Connecticut is **Waterbury**. It has a population of 107,174. It was first settled in 1674. The city became a manufacturing town, making clocks, watches, and pewter products. It was nicknamed "the brass city" because it was one of the largest manufacturers of products made out of that metal.

Republican American Tower at the train station in Waterbury.

Transportation

Connecticut's products were first transported by ship from port to port. In the 1800s, railroads helped to bring agricultural products and manufactured goods to other cities. Railroads thrived until automobiles became popular in the 1930s. Today, there are still passenger trains that go through Connecticut, mostly from Boston to New York City. Many Connecticut residents work in New York City. Since the highways are often busy, many people prefer to use trains.

The state has more than 20,000 miles (32,187 km) of roads and highways. Interstate 95 goes east and west along the coast. Interstate 91 goes north and south through Hartford. Other interstate highways crisscross the state.

Connecticut has more than 50 airports. Bradley International Airport, north of Hartford, is the state's busiest airport.

An Amtrak train travels near Mystic, Connecticut. Since the highways are often busy, many of Connecticut's residents prefer to travel by train.

Natural Resources

Connecticut has more than 4,000 farms. Dairy cows, chickens, and beef are big agricultural products. There are some small unique farms, too, where farmers raise alpacas, llamas, buffalo, and other animals. Crops include sweet corn, pears, apples, and tobacco.

A dairy farm in Lyme, Connecticut.

Shellfish farms off the coast bring money to the state. The fisheries of oysters, salmon, and shad were almost destroyed by pollution in the late 1900s. Over the last few decades, water quality improved and the fisheries made a comeback. Bluefish and striped bass are the main fish caught in Connecticut.

A lobster fisherman near Groton, Connecticut.

Iron and copper were mined in the state at the time of the Revolutionary War. Those mines closed long ago. Sand, stone, and clay are still mined today.

Industry

Prior to the Revolutionary War (1775–1783), Connecticut was a farm state. After the Revolutionary War, the state became known for its manufacturing. Many of its fast rivers were used to power machinery. Today, manufacturing is the main part of the state's economy. Manufactured items include machinery, electronics, and metal products. In the city of Groton, there is a large plant that builds submarines for the United States Navy.

The Seawolf-class submarine USS *Connecticut* was built in Groton, Connecticut.

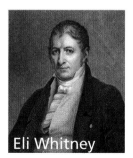
Eli Whitney

Eli Whitney was a Connecticut resident famous for building the cotton gin in 1793. "Gin" is short for "engine." The machine separated cotton's sticky seeds from its usable fibers. Whitney also created the idea of interchangeable parts during manufacturing.

The services part of Connecticut's economy is big and growing bigger. Services include insurance, finances, banking, and retail.

Tourism is also very important, earning $7 billion for the state each year. People come

A Connecticut covered bridge.

to see Connecticut's old historic buildings, as well as its beautiful hills and lakes. Resort areas along Long Island Sound are very popular.

Sports

Connecticut has no major-league professional football or baseball teams. However, there is professional

basketball. The Connecticut Sun is a team out of Uncasville that plays in the Women's National Basketball Association. Connecticut also has a number of minor league and development teams.

There are many outdoor recreational activities. The coastline along Long Island Sound is a popular place for boating and fishing. The state's heavily forested areas are good for hunting and wildlife watching. There are many places for camping and hiking as well.

Foxes are seen in forested areas.

Connecticut has more than 100 state parks and state forests. There are also many other parks and historical sites. Hammonasset Beach State Park, on the coast of Long Island Sound, is the largest public beach park.

With more than 2 miles (3 km) of beach, the popular Hammonasset Beach State Park is Connecticut's largest public beach park.

Entertainment

Connecticut has many different kinds of museums. The Wadsworth Atheneum, founded in 1842, is the oldest free public art museum in the United States. Yale University has its own art gallery. Yale is also home to the Peabody Museum of Natural History.

The Peabody Museum's display of deinonychus, a pack-hunting dinosaur with sickle-like claws. Deinonychus means "terrible claw."

Greenwich has the Bruce Museum of Arts and Sciences.

There are a number of theater groups in Connecticut. The Long Wharf Theater and the Yale Repertory Theater are both in New Haven. The Goodspeed Opera House puts on productions in East Haddam.

The Connecticut Scottish Festival celebrates the Scottish ancestry of many of the state's residents. Every October they play bagpipes, dance, and have other cultural celebrations.

Many tourists enjoy Mystic Seaport, a restored 1800s village.

Mystic Seaport, Connecticut

Timeline

1614—A Dutch explorer named Adriaen Block sails up the Connecticut River.

1635—Colonists move into the area, creating the first permanent English settlement.

1637–1638—A violent war erupts between New England settlers and the Pequot tribe. Many Pequot die or are captured and sold into slavery.

1638—Connecticut adopts the Fundamental Orders, the first state constitution.

1775–1783—Connecticut sends thousands of men to fight against England in the Revolutionary War.

1788—Connecticut becomes the fifth state.

1848—Connecticut abolishes slavery.

1861-1865—Connecticut supports the Union during the American Civil War.

1917-1918—Factories in Connecticut make military supplies to support the troops during World War I.

1929—The Great Depression begins. Many people in Connecticut are without jobs.

1941-1945—Connecticut sends thousands of soldiers to fight for their country during World War II. Submarines, airplane parts, and other military supplies made in Connecticut help the United States.

2004—University of Connecticut Huskies men's and women's basketball teams both win NCAA National Championship titles.

Glossary

Articles of Confederation—The written rules for the first United States government. It was approved by the original 13 states in 1781. The Articles of Confederation were replaced by the U.S. Constitution in 1789.

Civil War—The American war fought between the Northern and Southern states from 1861-1865. The Southern states were for slavery. They wanted to start their own country, known as the Confederacy. The Northern states fought against slavery and a division of the country.

Founding Fathers—The men who participated in the Constitutional Convention in 1787, especially the ones who signed the finished Constitution.

Fundamental Orders—A document that brought individual cities and villages together to form one unit. It functioned like a constitution to unite the people.

Long Island Sound—A bay of water that is part of the Atlantic Ocean. The sound is between Connecticut and New York's Long Island.

New England—An area in the northeast United States, consisting of the states of Maine, Vermont, New Hampshire, Massachusetts, Rhode Island, and Connecticut.

Panhandle—An area of land that juts out from the rest of the state. In Connecticut, there is a panhandle in the very southwest corner of the state.

Revolutionary War—The war fought between the American colonies and Great Britain from 1775-1783. It is also known as the War of Independence or the American Revolution.

World War I—A war that was fought in Europe from 1914 to 1918, involving countries around the world. The United States entered the war in April 1917.

World War II—A conflict across the world, lasting from 1939-1945. The United States entered the war in December 1941.

Index

A
Arizona 29
Arnold, Benedict 27
Articles of
    Confederation 27
Atlantic Coast 10
Atlantic Ocean 12

B
Bear Mountain 11
Block, Adriaen 18
Boston, MA 34
Bradley International
    Airport 35
Bridgeport, CT 30
Bruce Museum of Arts
    and Sciences 42

C
Candlewood, Lake 10
Canterbury, CT 26
Civil War 22
Congress, U.S. 25
Connecticut colony
    32
Connecticut
    Compromise 24,
    25
Connecticut River 10,
    18, 31
Connecticut River
    Valley 13
Connecticut Scottish
    Festival 43
Connecticut Sun 40
Constitution, U.S. 4,
    21
Constitutional
    Convention 24,
    25, 27
Coventry, CT 28
Crandall, Prudence 26

D
Danbury, CT 27
Darien, CT 29
Declaration of
    Independence 21,
    27

E
East Haddam, CT 43
England 21, 32

F
Founding Fathers 4
Frissell, Mount 11
Fundamental Orders 4

G
Goodspeed Opera
    House 43
Great Britain 28
Great Depression 22
Greenwich, CT 42
Groton, CT 38

H
Hale, Nathan 28
Hall, Richard Melville
    29
Hammonasset (tribe)
    18
Hammonasset Beach
    State Park 41
Hartford, CT 18, 19,
    29, 31, 34, 35
Hartford Conservatory
    31
House of
    Representatives,
    U.S. 25

L
Long Island Sound 8,
    17, 32, 39, 40, 41
Long Wharf Theater 43

M
Maine 8
Massachusetts 8,
    11, 19
Melville, Herman 29
Meyer, Stephenie 29
Moby 29
Moby-Dick 29
Mohegan (tribe) 18
Mystic Seaport 43

N
Navy, U.S. 38
New England 8, 10
New Hampshire 8
New Haven, CT 32
New York 8, 29
New York City, NY 8,
    34
Nipmuc (tribe) 18
Norwich, CT 27

P
Peabody Museum of
    Natural History 42
Pequannock (tribe)
    30
Pequot (tribe) 18, 20
Pequot War 20
Puritans 32

Q
Quinnipiac (tribe) 18

R
Revolutionary War
    21, 27, 37, 38
Rhode Island 8

S
Senate, U.S. 25
Sherman, Roger 25,
    27
Sicaog (tribe) 31

T
Twilight 29

U
Uncasville, CT 40
Union 22
United States 4, 8,
    21, 22, 24, 25, 42
University of
    Bridgeport 30
University of
    Hartford 31

V
Vermont 8

W
Wadsworth Atheneum
    42
Waterbury, CT 33
Whitney, Eli 39
Winthrop, John 19
Women's National
    Basketball
    Association 40
World War I 22
World War II 23

Y
Yale Repertory
    Theater 43
Yale University 28,
    32, 42